MY ANGELS FOLLOW ME EVERYWHERE

For my Sweet Baby Angel, Mia.

~ J.K.

For my daughter, Alesha.

~ D.R.

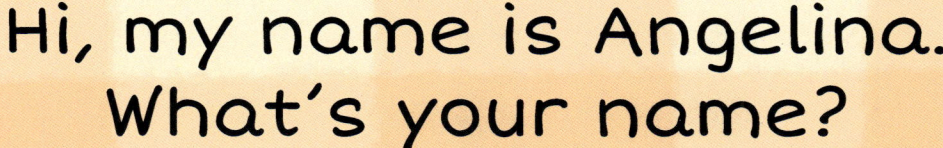

Hi, my name is Angelina.
What's your name?

I can't see my angels, but I know they are there. I can feel their love in my heart.

When I was born, two angels appeared. You have angels too!

They always stay close to me. Your angels stay close to you too!

My angels come to school with me.
They can hear
my whispers,
even on
a noisy
bus.

What will you whisper to your angels?

Our angels understand every language around the world. They listen to the feelings we hold in our heart.

My mom talks to her angels out loud all the time. She even asks her angels to help us find a good parking spot!

"Thank you, angels." Mom always says.

There are
many ways
to talk to
angels.

Did you
talk to
your
angels
today?

Your angels are always happy to help you.

Remember to thank your angels for their help!

When I go to the park, I like to climb all the way to the top of the jungle gym.

I feel brave and strong because my angels remind me to hold on tight.

My angels can move so fast!

When I'm speeding down the path on my bike, I can feel them going just as fast as me!

Sometimes, I get the feeling to slow down before it's too late.

One time, I was going so fast that I almost fell off my bike! It was scary for a moment, but I have a feeling that my angels helped me get my balance again.

What do you think?

When I'm playing hide-and-seek, my angels like to play along with me.

They don't mind squeezing into small spaces.

There's always room for an angel!

My angels follow me because it is their special job to help protect me and keep me safe. I have to listen when they warn me when danger is near.

"Thank you, angels." I say to them.

If you ever feel scared or sad, you can ask your angels to help your heart feel happy again.

Hold your arms out, and imagine giving your angels a big hug.

Even if you can't see them, they are hugging you back!

Grandma says she has angels too. She told me angels don't grow old. Grandma says angels don't get hungry or sleepy either.

Have you ever woken up in the middle of the night? My angels are always by my side to comfort me, and help me fall asleep again.

My angels are always there for me when I need them. Your angels are always there for you too!

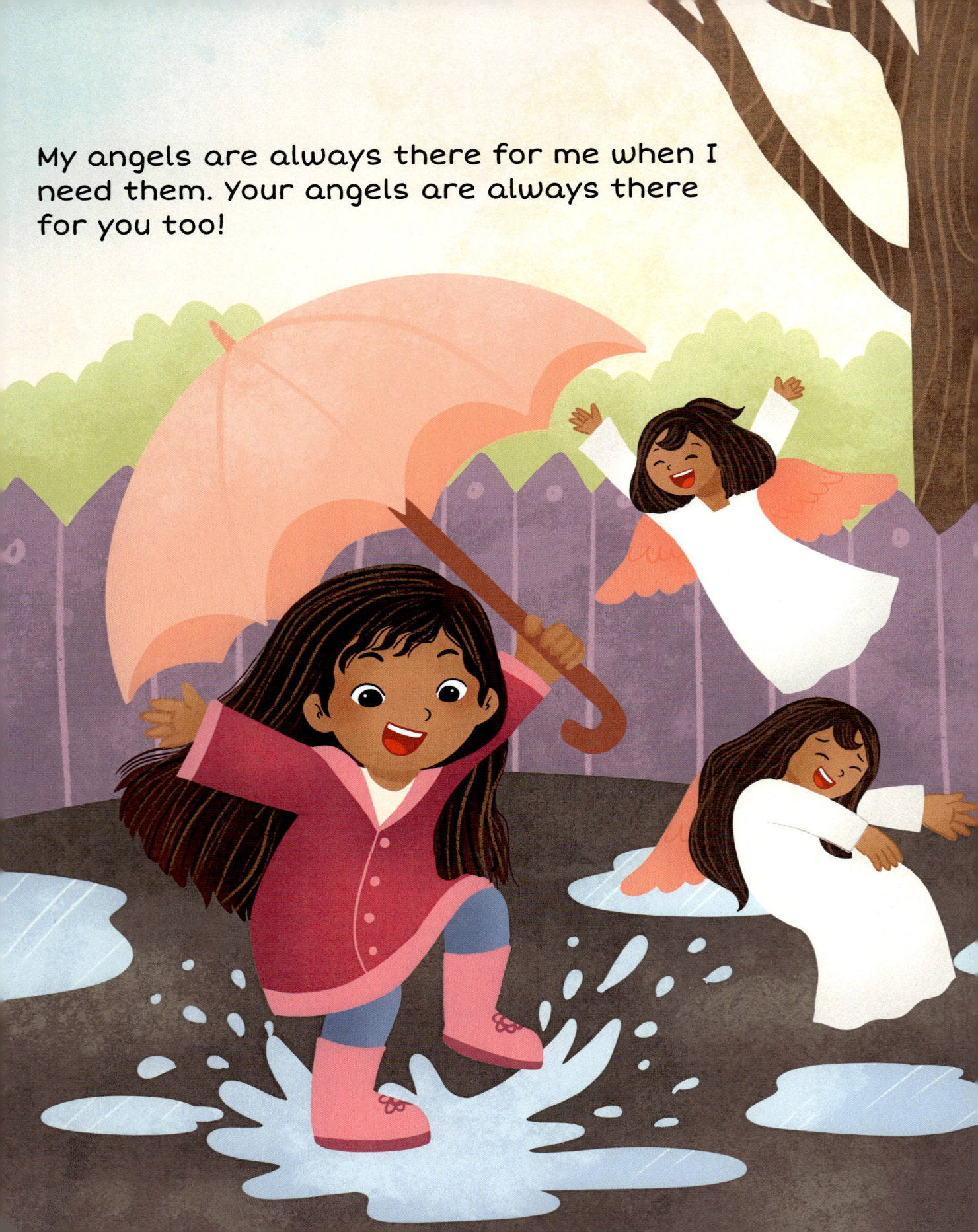

You can ask your angels anything. They always hear you.

Listen with your heart to what they are telling you.

What names should I give my angels?

What names will
you choose for
your angels?

About the Author

Jennifer Krejci is a preschool teacher, and a life-long student of metaphysics. She has been an intuitive empath since early childhood. This is her first self-published children's book.

About the Illustrator

Debby Rahmalia grew up with the love of art. She has actively participated in art competitions from national to international levels since she was a child. Now she spends her time illustrating children's books. Visit her on: www.instagram.com/debbyrahmalia

Made in the USA
Monee, IL
26 January 2021